2020 Editor's Note

This book has a special place in my heart. I did not realize when I was younger looking through all the books my grandma and dad had written in our old family store that one day, I would start my career at this national park site. I vaguely remember the first time I stumbled across this book and read about the rivers.

Looking back now, I wish I asked Grandma and Grandpa why they never did a second edition or updated it at all. I did ask Dad when I started to work on republishing the books and he said that life got busy for everyone and grandma was working on some of her other books. They talked about redoing it a few times but never seemed to come together on it.

During the republishing process, and seeing how much has changed over the years, this book will be revised. I will do a revised edition later this year to address some minor errors, historical relevance, and expand on areas of interest—and update photos!

The photos killed me; they are from the original book but when you photocopy photocopies you lose so much detail. The only major change is the price of the book and some medical information. In 1967, the book cost $1.00. Due to the rise in inflation this book would cost $7.79 in today's money. For ease of access, there will be an ebook for $3.99 and the paperback for $6.99.

    -Bobbie Roshone

    JP Brand Books

Ozark National Scenic Riverways

This book is dedicated to the good Ozark people who gave up their homes to make this park possible.

The authors,

D.D., Eunice & Albert Pennington

Copyright 1967

©Albert Pennington

*Copies of this book may be obtained by sending $1. to the Pennington Trading Post, Fremont, Mo. 63941.

JP Brand Books
Read the Brand

*Original printing, Pennington Trading Post is permanently closed.

Dedication

As this book goes to press development has not yet started on the Ozark Scenic Riverways park but 98% of the proposed 65,000 acres is now under contract for appraisal or has already been appraised. The first edition of this book is a limited one. Future editions will be revised to include developments in the park as they occur.

Proposed plans call for 14 access points for boat launching, 10 campgrounds, 13 picnic areas, 7 ranger stations, 15 interpretive areas and two ferries.
There is to about 100 miles of hiking and horseback trails. There will be approximately 20 miles of access roads.

The rivers can now be floated but everything is yet in the wild. There are only a few camp sites that are even considered to have primitive accommodations.
Canoe rentals will be with private individuals throughout the Riverways. The guides will also be employed on a private basis.

Folks who select to make the float in their own canoes without guide service should seek information from local tourist information centers and from the Ozark National Scenic Riverways office located at Van Buren. The Lands Division of the Riverways is located in Eminence, Mo.

Facilities and programs will be developed to promote such activities as boating, fishing, hunting, swimming, camping, picnicking, golfing, leisure Motoring, horseback riding, hiking, nature studies, museum, and campfire interpretive programs, guided and self-guiding nature tours, and an interpretation of early Ozark Folk culture.

Map 1.1

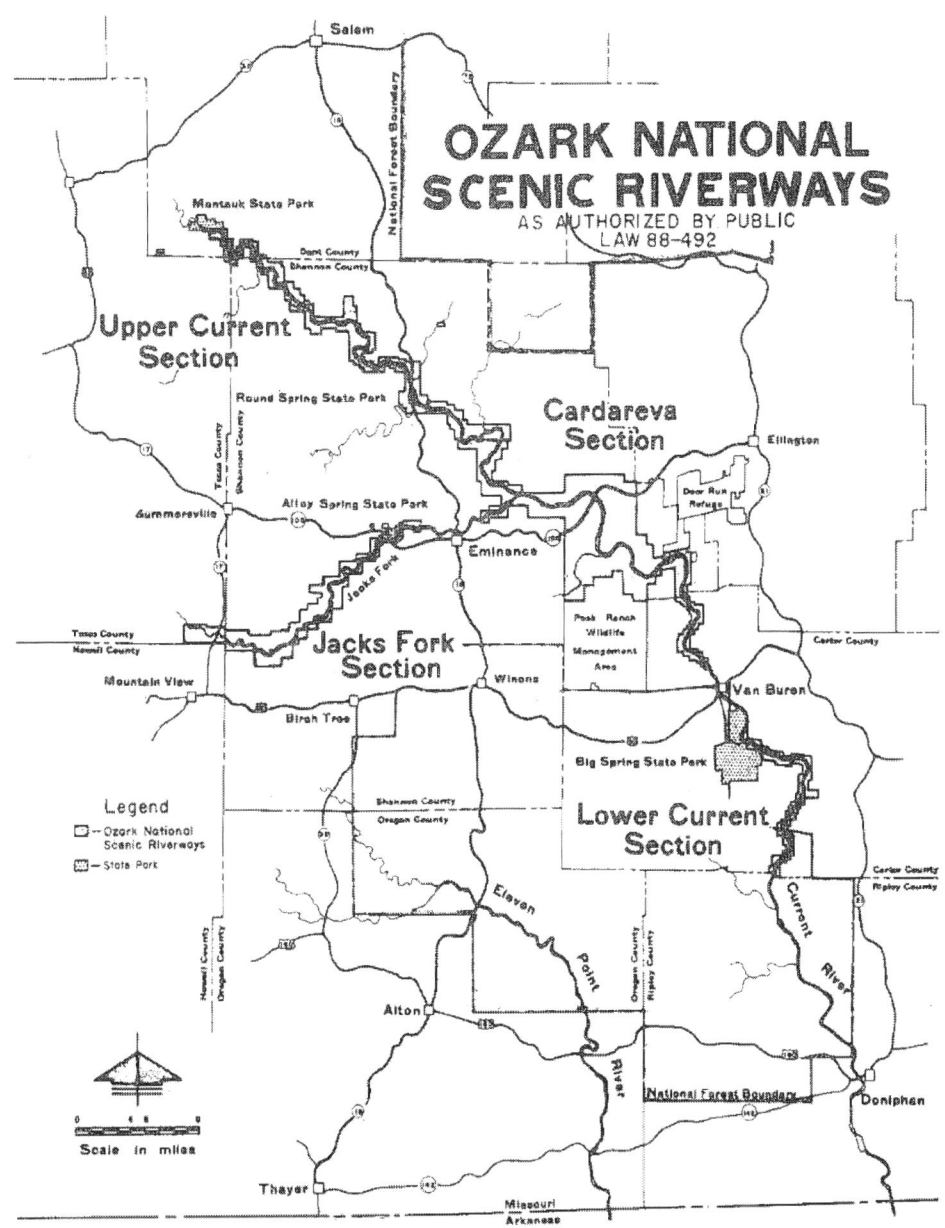

"This map shows the park as authorized. Part of the land to be included in the Ozark Riverways is still in private ownership and is not open to the public."

Map 1.2

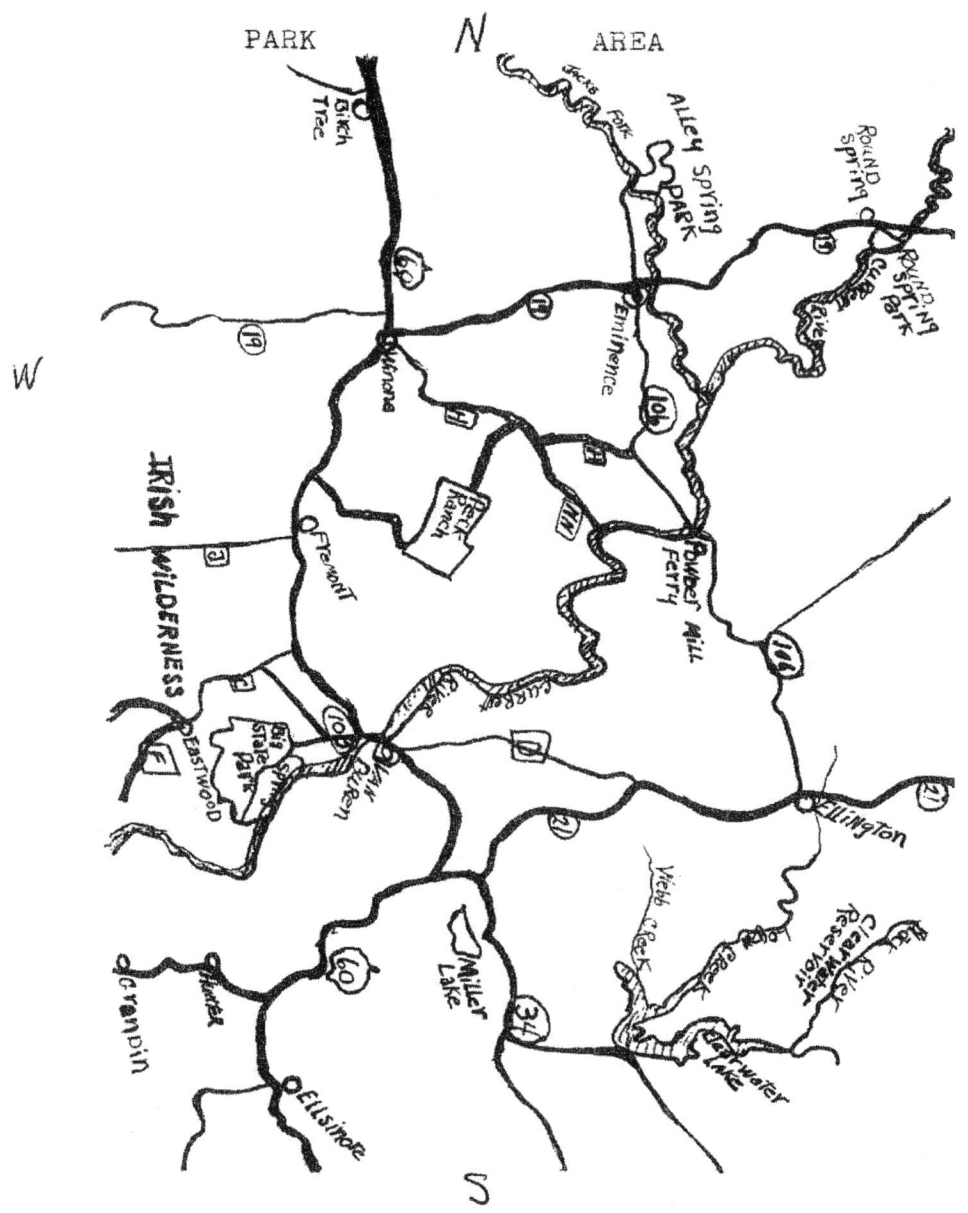

Table of Contents

2020 Editor's Note 1
Dedication 4
Map 1.1 5
Map 1.2 6
Table of Contents 7
List of Illustrations 8
Preface 10
The Ozarks 11
Ozark National Scenic Riverways 12
The Rivers 13
Geology and Hydrology 15
Climate 17
Soils 18
Plant Life 19
Harmful Plants 22
Livestock 23
Wildlife 24
History 40
Places in the Park 55
Recreation 58
MARK TWAIN NATIONAL FOREST 63
Surroundings 64
Places of Interest 70
Park Formation 71
BIBLIOGRAPHY 72
Index 73
The Authors 77

List of Illustrations

Plant Life... 19-20

   Livestock...22

Animal Life..30-35

Historical Pictures...........................49-53

   Recreational Pictures....................62-63

   Other Places to See......................65-71

Original Cover 1967

Thank you from the Pennington Books Project

Preface

The purpose of this publication is to give the visitor a guide to the Ozark Scenic Riverways and a glimpse into the historical background of the region.

The recreational outlets are listed. The places to see, trails to follow, and the campsites are given. Nearby attractions are listed along with some of their history and legend.

The historical part of the book has been included to help the visitor understand why such a great wilderness section has remained almost as wild as nature made it. There is a marked relationship between the early folk who first came here and those who claim to be the natives living here now. These folks have made a great unselfish sacrifice in giving up their secluded homes for a park that will be a joy and pleasure to many generations to come.

We are indebted to many fine people who helped us in the compiling and editing of this book.

Along the agencies who assisted were: The National Park Service, The National Forest Service, The Missouri Conservation Commission, and the State Historical Society of Missouri.

We expect that some changes will be made in the original plans of the Ozark National Scenic Riverways before the park is completed. For that reason, this will be a limited edition so that in the event of any changes they can be reckoned with in future printings.

The Ozarks

You've come to an unusual place—the Ozarks. This Mountain range is not of unusual height or shape. It appears to be made up of huge bumps sticking out of the earth's surface. Nearly all the Mountains are covered in timber growth. The only exceptions being surfaces where limestone outcrops appear or where man has cleared away the timber.

In late spring and early summer, a parade of colors awaits the visitor. This entire area is a lovely paradise resembling a wildflower garden.

In mid-winter it's a bleak, desolate appearing Mountain land. A snow cover or an ice sheet can suddenly change it into a shimmering winter wonderland.

The autumn is indeed a show, with its gorgeous colors. To really see and to appreciate its grandeur, the visitor should return at intervals for observing and noting the difference that each change of season produces.

Ozarka grows on one. At first you may only see the beauty of the far-off Mountains or if you come for your fist visit in winter their bleakness may stun you.

The oftener you come and the longer you stay helps create in you a real feeling of relaxation and a state of mind known as Ozarka. There is no obvious hurry to the routine of the Ozark people. They all seem to have a goal and a purpose to their work, but it does not have the driving force that appears in the cities.

Ozark National Scenic Riverways

Ozark National Scenic Riverways is administered by the National Park Service. It is located in the Ozark Mountain section of south-central Missouri. It is an elongated stretch of land lying on both sides of two free-flowing wild rivers.

The Current River and its largest tributary, the Jacks Fork are the scene of this new park. The Riverways includes approximately 140 lineal miles along the banks of these two beautiful streams.

The park encompasses that portion of the Current extending from Montauk Spring in Dent County in a southeasterly direction about 101 miles to the Carter-Ripley county line, and that portion of the Jacks Fork extending from a point about 3 miles west of Missouri 17 in Texas County in a northeasterly direction about 39 miles to Alley Spring. The total area will include about 86,000 acres.

This park is in the central part of the United States. It is 175 miles southwest of St. Louis, 270 miles west of Nashville, 300 miles southeast of Kansas City, only 145 miles east of Springfield, 180 miles northwest of Memphis, and 50 miles west of Poplar Bluff.

Ozark National Scenic Riverways is the first Riverways to be included in the National Park system. This area was authorized under public law 88-482, signed into law by President Lyndon B. Johnson on August 27, 1964. The area will be administered by the National Park Service, U.S. Department of the Interior. Land acquisition began in 1966.

The Rivers

The Current and Jacks Fork Rivers are still in a primitive wild state. Some farms lie along their banks, but little has been done by man to mar their natural beauty. By floating these rivers one can see nature at its best. Both rivers are fast flowing and rugged.

Many scenic spots can be seen from automobiles. Various camping sites may be reached by vehicles. Other means such as horseback riding and hiking can be resorted too, in an effort to see the secluded spots that are not yet accessible by roads.

There is no doubt that Current River got its name from its swift and treacherous current. It is said that the Indians told the French about the current of this turbulent stream before white men ever saw it. The French were in Missouri as early as 1673.

Current River has a larger low water discharge flow than any other river in this state. It falls at the rate of seven feet per mile. It is navigable with canoes at all seasons. This very crooked stream served as the only transportation outlet for this area for many years. Besides, transportation the river furnished power for the grinding of corn, and for the making of lumber.

The Jacks Fork of the Current gets its name from a captain of Revolutionary War fame, who later settled here. The Jacks Fork is a much smaller stream, although, it is also characterized by its swift, wild current. Even during the early spring when Jacks Fork carries an abundance of water it is a tamer river to float than the Current. When the river is low the Jacks Fork does not afford the canoeist with complete clearance for floating over all shoals.

Floating the rivers is the best way to get close to nature. This was the same method used by early hunters who first braved the wilds.

La Hontan, a Frenchman, was the first known white man to brave the Missouri wilderness as a hunter. Little is known about his explorations, but it is believed that he might have penetrated this region at least to the fringe of the Ozarks near the headwaters of the Current.

The boundaries of the Ozark region have never been defined; however, it has become an established practice to include the St. Francois, Boston, and Ouachita ranges when speaking of the Ozarks.

Some historians believe that the creation of the word "Ozarks" derived from the term "auz arcs" which is a name once applied to the bow-hunting tribe of Quapaw Indians. These Indians often used the Mountains here as their tribal hunting grounds.

The mainstream of migration westward passed to the north and south of this part of the Ozarks leaving them almost unexplored for over half a century after settlements had been made farther to the north and west.

During this half-century, the Mountains here were consider a sort of no man's land. Wandering Indian bands still came here to hunt. Outlaws consider it a safe place to rendezvous. Explorers sought to roam the great western country for More adventures.

Geology and Hydrology

The Ozarks are the oldest Mountain range in the world. Actually, it is a geographical section made up of rolling hills, swiftly flowing streams, and rugged forests.

The rock formations are probably over a half-a-billion years old. The More recent deposits of sediments probably came from the oceans that once covered the land.

Since the land emerged from the ocean, erosion has been busy all through the years wearing down the Mountainside while building up deposits of sandstone and limestone.

The entire Ozark Plateau is undermined with a network of hidden water courses ranging from small trickling streams to deep underground rivers. Some of these water courses come boiling to the surface, clear and cold. The temperature of the water and the gaseous radio activity signifies the Ozark water sources are very deep inside the earth's surface.

The Most logical theory seems to be that this huge amount of water comes from very deep underground pools brought to the earth's surface by tremendous pressure from the earth's weight. Water from the oceans fill the underground caverns. While on its long route from the sea it becomes purified and freed from much of its salt. The time involved in this process maybe a matter of several years.

This is only a theory, but it becomes More logical in meaning when we think what an enormous amount of water that flows from the More than 500 major springs in the Ozarks.

We know that for ages underground streams have been flowing because their partially abandoned channels constitute over 1500 known caves. The water courses are gradually changing but man's lifetime is so short that we not become aware of the constant geophysical shift that is taking place all around us.

In this limestone region springs are very abundant. Most of the springs are pure and free of mineral matter. The water of many of these springs are claimed to be of healthful value while some contain a small salt content.

Most of the springs flow remarkable cold water which may be contributed to the great depth of the water sources.

Numerous strange phenomena in the way of springs and wells exist. There are big springs, falling springs, ebb and flow springs, dripping springs, boiling springs, sand springs, blue springs, still springs, and hidden springs. Why so many varied features and unusual phenomenon about springs? Why is Blue Spring always blue? Why does Big Spring flow such great quantities of water? Why does a dripping spring drip? What causes the continual boiling of sand in Sands Spring? What causes the ebb and flow of some springs? Why do some springs appear to be calm while others come dashing forth almost like a fountain?

The stories and legends connected with the springs of this region make up a whole book.

Climate

The climate of the Ozark region cannot be surpassed in any other Mountain area in the United States. We have an average of 275 days of sunshine yearly. The average temperature is 65 degrees. The average winter temperature is 35 degrees while the average summer temperature is 80 degrees.

The rainfall averages about 35 inches but it is not well distributed. Droughts are one of the Most dreaded difficulties faced by the Ozark farmer.

The Mountains are high enough to affect the climate locally. They ward off the cold winter, western winds. During the summer, the heat waves pass around the Mountains both to the north and south of the Ozarks.

Actually, the variation in surface and difference in altitude tend to bring about certain variations in climate in the Mountains. It has often been said that one can find almost any kind of climate in the Ozarks.

The Ozarks are considered a haven of refuge for those seeking retirement or the restoration of health. This is due to the fact that the weather seldom gets extremely hot or extremely cold. Back away from the streams a drier type of climate may be enjoyed. Morning fogs are often prevalent along the streams and on the big lakes.

The purple appearing mist or haze that appears so often in the park is another of nature's mysteries which has not yet been solved. The mist usually appears in early Morning or in the late afternoons.

Soils

The soils in the Ozark region are varied. A very small percent along the creeks and rivers is classified as Huntington. It is suited for extensive cropping as it is well drained. This type has a deep topsoil with a clay subsoil base. It responds to the use of commercial fertilizers as well as any soil in the U.S. Yields of 100 bushels of corn per acre is not uncommon. Also, good alfalfa is produced on this limited acreage.

Our next best soil is classified as Linside which is not as productive as the Huntington. It contains some rock or gravel but is used extensively for cropping. However, it is better suited to the production of grasses, legumes, and forage crops.

A small part of the upland is quite productive when fertilized and protected from erosion. The greatest precent of our soil is known as Clarksville, which is suited primarily to timber production as it is too stony, steep, and dry to cultivate.

Most of the bottom soils are subject to overflow because our hills are so steep. The soil is not undulated for long.

Our topsoil is quite rich in minerals and produces the best hardwood oak for flooring in the world. The best wood for the production of handles is found here. For this reason, tree farming has emerged here in recent years. Great stands of shortleaf pine have been seeded throughout the hills.

Plant Life

The plant life of the Ozarks is a subject of worldwide interest among botanists. These hills are the meeting place of the northern hardwoods and the southern pines. There are so many variations of the over 1500 different species of plant life in the region that the students here find it of great interest. The Most challenging formation is the repestrine, which is a name applied to the whole vegetation found growing upon rocks and cliffs.

Some plants were brought to this area by the settlers, while all the others grew wild in the forests. The huge native pine trees measured from three to five feet in diameter and from twenty-five to ninety feet in height.

The cutting of the great forest brought to this region many people from all walks of life, from many different nationalities and cultures. Some stayed on to manufacture the timber. The harvesting of the great forest right at the turn of the century was really responsible for further industrialization of this section.

Millions of dollars' worth of timber was cut. Also, of much value has been the herbs of medical nature taken from the woods. At critical times, wild Ginseng roots have been known to sell for sixteen dollars per pound.

Wild fruit bearing trees, berries, and grapes provide food for wildlife. Acorns and nuts from the trees add to the food supply for animals and birds.

The Sassafras of the region has been sent to all parts of the word to be used as a tea herb, for oil, medicine, and perfumery. It is also used in the soft drink industry.

Many beautiful wildflowers abound in the park. From early spring until autumn some flowers are blooming at all times. A few of these flowers are so rare as to be found growing only in the Ozarks. One of the rarest and Most unusual wildflower is the Ozark Orchid known as "Lady Slipper."

Flowering trees such as the Dogwood, Redbud, Wild Plum, and Hawthorne have been written about by our poets. Springtime is a festive season and an ideal time to visit the park to see the trees in their gay arrays.

Autumn too, is a season of enchantment with the late blooming flowers such as the Golden Rod, Corn Flowers, and Asters.

No other Mountain region in the world can boast of its fall coloration of the leaves as can the Ozarks. The trees here present such flaming gay fall colors as pinks, deep reds, variegated yellows, oranges, and browns.

Scientists believe that the chlorophyll, which gives the leaf its green coloring, gradually disappears. Then gradually, the gay colored carotenoids appear and multiply. As More carotenoids grow the brown pigments, known as tannins, replace the green chlorophyll as the time approaches for the leaves to fall.

Anthocyanins are the pigments that give the leaves the gorgeous dark hues from scarlet through the violets to blue. Just how these pigments are formed and why some seasons produce lovelier leaves than others have the scientists and other nature lovers guessing.

Some folks claim that the early frost hastens the development of the pigments, causing the colorful seasons to the last only a few days. Others maintain that the amount of sunlight hastens the maturation of the leaves. They feel that damp cloudy weather in September followed by a killing frost will keep the leaves from falling early and make for a long season of lingering beauty.

The approximate date of this flaming fall revenue of colors is from October 10 to November 1. This time may vary slightly from year to year depending somewhat on the weather conditions that prevail. This beautiful season brings thousands of people to the hills to view the colors and watch the changes that occur during the process.

Many unusual plants grow in the Ozarks. One that brings visitors to the hills in the springtime is the lovely rose Azalea or "wild honeysuckle" whose botanical name is Rhododendron Roseum. The Ozarks is the only section of the state where rose Azalea thrives. The rocky hillsides provide the acid soils upon which the azalea thrives.

Other unusual trees or bushes appear here. They bear folk names such as pawpaw, skunkbrush, ironwood, slippery elm, spicewood, buckbrush and brome siege.

Most of the forest trees consists of several varieties of each of the common oak, pine, willow, walnut, cottonwood, hickory, hazel, birch, alder, chinkapin, elm, hackberry, mulberry, sycamore, hawthorne, redbud, dogwood, sumac, maple, buckeye, thorn, gum, ash, elder, haw, persimmon, and poplar.

Abundant water plants--scene at peck Ranch

Forested hills--scene at Van Buren

Harmful Plants

A few of the plants growing here are harmful to man. The cruelness of nature seems to place them near the very pathways by which human beings are Most likely to travel.

The Most dreaded is Poison Ivy. It can be detected by its three leaf groupings. More people are affected by its poisonous rash each year than by any other obnoxious plant. The vines of ivy cling to trees, fences, and buildings for support.

Poison Mushrooms: Visitors should not eat mushrooms and toadstools that appear in the woods at any time or for any reason. You will see various books and guides describing to you the eatable varieties; however, drought and floods may affect the mushroom's edibility. Some of the Most poisonous mushrooms in the world appear here at intervals. The risk involved is not worth the few bites of tasty spores that might take your life before your meal is finished. The wisest rule to follow is gather none—eat none.

Wild garlic, wild onions and sheep sorrel are all favorite plants to cut and add to campside meals, however, growing in the same type of soil and exposure is the deadly crow-poison feared throughout the Ozarks by the natives.

Visitors are advised not to pluck greens either to eat raw or cooked. It is far cheaper and such safer to purchase both your greens and mushrooms from the supermarkets.

Harmful Weeds:

Dog fennel and jimson: These two weeds are enticing to children because of their gay flowers. They are found growing along roadsides and in abandoned fields. Either one can be the cause of great discomfort should the fumes or juice get into a person's eyes, nose, or Mouth.

Visitors are also warned not to pluck small wild fruits or berries for eating purposes for among the edible ones are also some that are dangerous. The poisonous nightshade, while not classified as a fruit or a vegetable can easily be confused as such, by a child. The pokeberry, wild cherry and some grape-like appearing fruits are harmful.

Livestock

Farming and stock rising are still carried on near the park. Except for lumbering it has been the Ozark way of life for over a century. Agriculture still ranks near the top as a leading industry here. Better farming methods coupled with the use of purebred breeding stock has brough about great changes in agriculture during the past two decades. The widespread use of commercial fertilizers, the establishment of permanent pastures, flood control and reforestation have all helped to make the farm a better place to live.

The area here is particularly noted for its production of fine feeder pigs and feeder cattle. Horses, mostly of the pleasure type are produced here. Other farm animals include sheep, goats, and dogs. Dogs, especially the hound and faithful farm dog, hold a distinguished place in Ozark History.

Feeder cattle

Mother sheep with triplett lambs

A horse for every purpose produced here, from the minature shetland to saddle hor

Paper carrier

A range sow

A trained cat

Faithful farm dog

A purebred walker

Milk Goats

23

Wildlife

The Ozark region is a natural habitat for wildlife and produces a wide variety of interesting animals.

The area is well watered, produces an abundance of food for wildlife, has no severe climatic conditions and is well covered in timber habitats. All these features add up to an animal haven.

Harvesting of wildlife here has been going on for almost 200 years yet it continues to reproduce and replenish somewhat the various species. Through the patient work of the Missouri Conservation Commission these Mountains still produce an abundance of deer, squirrels, rabbits, raccoons, skunks, opossums, and beaver. Other protected wildlife includes weasels, muskrats, civic cats, and mink.

It has not yet been necessary to put a closed season on bobcats, groundhogs, foxes, and coyotes. There is no open season on the scarcer species of the bear, otter, and badger.

The advent of the farm pond has greatly added to the survival element in the production of wildlife. The Ozarks are considered a well-watered region, which is very true, but in extremely droughty seasons water holes are so far apart that small animals often fail to survive.

Another factor that has helped in replenishing the small game species is the combination of farms under one-man ownership. Better farming practices are being adhered too with More cover crops, and More permanent pastures being seeded.

Deer:

The best known and Most talked about animal in the Ozark National Scenic Riverways Park is the White-tailed deer. Named for its flashy white tail, it presents a dramatic picture as it dashes away into the woods.

The Ozarks provide a natural habitat for the deer because of the ideal climate here, the abundant supplies of food, the heavy foliage for cover, and a peaceful place in which to reproduce its young. The food for deer consists of acorns, nuts, berries, farm crops of all kinds, and all types of vegetation.

Deer are well camouflaged in this environment. The buck can be distinguished during summer by his rack of antlers, while the does have none. The fawns are born in early spring. They are quite spotted at birth. They are usually born in pairs; however, a doe may give birth to only one or as many as three. The fawns lose their spots when they are five or six Months old. Deer usually band together in small family groups. Except at breeding time, only a few stays in a herd.

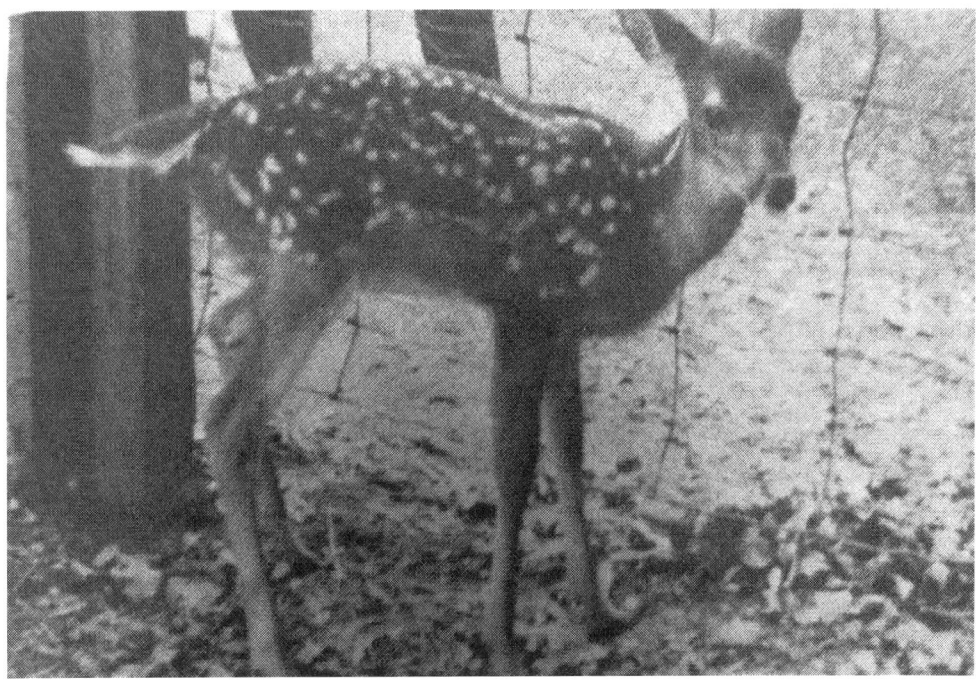

"Fawn at the age of six weeks."

Bear:

The black bear is the largest wild animal we have in the hills at this time. When grown they weigh between 200 and 600 pounds. Compared to a hog, the bear has a massive head, round ears, and a dog type nose. The bear has powerful jaws, a bull type neck with big shoulders. He has excellent hearing and smelling senses but rather poor eyesight. The bear has a strong leg, and huge paws with five toes on each foot. His long sharp claws serve as dangerous weapons which he also uses to help him climb. He can climb exceptionally well for his bulky size.

The bear is a traveler, constantly in search of food except for his short interval of hibernation. In summer, the bear feeds on insects of all kinds as well as rodents, fish, fruit, and carrion. In winter he hibernates for a period of time starting about midwinter. He chooses to sleep in a secluded cave. The Ozarks provide this natural habitat for the bear.

The bear does not present a grave danger to man. He is naturally afraid of man and if unmolested will go away peacefully. However, children should be warned that in the event they suddenly encounter a bear to drop whatever food they may be carrying and stay completely away from the animal. If Molested or teased the bear will naturally try to protect himself. Because of his greedy nature the smell of food may cause him to follow a person who is carrying candy or other sweet-smelling foods. Only a few bears live in the park, but children should be constantly reminded that they might come upon one unexpectantly.

Raccoon:

The raccoon with its comical mask is to be found throughout the hardwood forest of the park area. Contrary to popular belief, the raccoon does not always wash his food before eating it. His diet varies and depends on the season. During summer he may feed around the creeks, fishing, and frogging. During the cold winter Months, the raccoon seeks the high ridges where he feeds on acorns, and grubs.

The raccoon's diet during the year consists of acorns, grubs, snails, mice, squirrels, rabbits, muskrats, snakes, night crawlers, birds and their eggs, berries, corn, wild cherries, apples, persimmons, lizards, fish, frogs, crawfish, bugs, paw-paws, grapes, and vegetables. These cunning animals often come into the campsites by night to search for scraps left by visitors.

Raccoons usually feed at night and are seldom seen in daytime. The raccoon likes to take a sunbath during the late autumn, winter, and early spring. Watch for him during the time of mid-day. He may be sleeping on a high limb of a tree where the sun will shine on him. His color will blend well with the oak tree bark. It requires close observation to get to see him.

Wild Hogs:

A few wild hogs live in the park area. These beasts are the Most dangerous of any animal living wild in this region. So, few are they in number that visitors will seldom see them. If by chance the visitor should come in contact with a wild hog, he had best remain calm and seek the protection of the nearest car.

SQUIRRELS:

There are four well known species of squirrels found in the park. The red or Fox squirrel is the largest and probably covers the widest range. It inhabits the ridge tops and higher ground. The Fox Squirrel depends on the mast for Most of its food supply. For that reason, their numbers are variable.

The Gray Squirrel is a smaller, swift running little animal that habitats the low bottomlands, especially along the streams. The Gray Squirrel takes to the trees when pursued. It can leap from tree to tree in the dense forest as a means of eluding its enemies.

The Chipmunk is the tiny striped back squirrel that scurries about among the rocks and boulders. He may choose a hole in a hollow stump or burrow for his home. Because it always dwells in or near the ground, it is often called the "Ground Squirrel." The Chipmunk's diet is much the same as other squirrels, but he can live on much less because of his small size.

The Flying Squirrel is seldom seen because it "stirs" Mostly by night. It lives in secluded areas of the park. The Flying Squirrel is small, and very stout with unusual side muscles that makes gliding possible. The Flying Squirrel can easily glide for from ten to twenty fee and can do so with remarkable speed. Both the Flying Squirrel and the Chipmunk hibernate for short periods of time during the winter.

Migration of squirrels is not unusual in the Ozarks. Both Red and Gray Squirrels are known to migrate when food supplies are short.

Other Animals:

There are two kinds of skunks in the Ozarks. The Most numerous is the striped skunk, whose coloration is from that of the broad white stripe to solid black. The skunk dens in ground holes, logs, and among limestone boulders. If Molested, it gives off a very unpleasant odor.

Another kind of skunk is the spotted skunk or civic cat. This little creature has habits somewhat like the striped skunk. His odor is even More unpleasant. The fur is very soft and lovely (picture on pg. 39).

The Ozark area is known for the fine crop of cottontail rabbits which it produces annually. Watch for the rabbits along the country roadsides in late afternoon.

The western coyote came into the Ozarks upon the replenishment of the deer herds. Both coyotes and wolves appeared here awhile. We now have a mixture. In some areas both species are reported to appear.

Two species of the cat family live here. The bobcat is the Most common. Named for its stubby, short tail, the bobcat is a fierce fighter and preys on smaller animals (picture pg. 39). The wildcat is less numerous. It has the same bad habits and is very difficult to track down and kill.

The beaver, a rodent, lives near the water. He is a dam builder and vegetarian (see pictures of his work on pg. 30-31).

The mink a small fur bearing animal lives in a bank den but prefers to take his food from the streams. The mink's fur is very valuable. Very few minks live in this area and are seldom seen.

Tree notched by beaver in the process of dam building.

Dam across Barren Creek made by beaver.

A tree cut down by beaver

Red or Fox Squirrel--a natural tree planter

red fox   gray fox

Black Bear feasting on garbage

The weasel is a tiny animal a wee bit larger than a rat. He lives in a bank den but feeds on water animals. The weasel will also eat food scraps and raid the hen house.

Only a few river otters exist here. The otter lives in bank dens with entrances below the surface. They spend their time in the den or under water. They are seldom seen except by scuba divers.

Several species of rat live here. The muskrat is the best known. It dens along streams and ponds and spends a great deal of its time in the water. A Most unusual animal is the packrat. It spends its short life dragging and carrying objects to its den. One den examined contained 61 different objects that had been taken from a nearby farm.

Several species of mice dwell here. The white-footed filed Mouse is the Most common. The shrew is often mistaken for a Mouse because of its size. It Moves at great speed and is More destructive.

Various kinds of lizards can be seen among the rocks and old logs. The Most common is the gray lizard, however, a lovely blue lizard maybe seen as well as the red lizard.

Bats are found in the caves here. In late afternoon they may be seen outside while feeding on the wing. Sometimes they choose to feed in early Morning before the sun comes up. Bats seem to have no distinct vision. They guide themselves with a unique instinctive device that no other mammal seems to possess.

HARMFUL CREATURES:

Stinging scorpions: These slimy looking creatures can be distinguished by their up curled tails that carry a long stinger in the end. While the sting is seldom fatal, they are extremely painful. The best first aid treatment is the ice pack applied directly to the wound.

Leach: This tiny water animal will fasten itself to the flesh of humans and cling in a sucking manner to the skin. While the leach is not considered dangerous, the injury can be painful and can become infected.

Ticks: These small creatures attack both man and beast. To visitors there appears to be several different species, however, the tick goes through several changes in size and appearance during its life cycle. A drop of turpentine on the tick will make it turn loose from the flesh.[1] The turpentine also acts as a cleanser for the wound. Infected tick bites should be treated by a physician.

Chiggers: These are the little red mites that appear on the flesh and cause great discomfort. Lindane dusted on shoes and trouser leges is the best preventative.

Spiders: Many spiders live in the Ozarks. The Merry Widow whose bites is sometimes fatal to man is the Most dangerous. This spider can be recognized by its shiny black body and a bright red spot on its belly. In case of bite the victim should be rushed to a doctor. The tarantula is not really considered a venomous spider, but it should be treated carefully because some fatalities have been reported in the past from neglected bites.

Flying Stinging Pests: The wasp, yellowjacket, hornet, honeybee, bumble bee and sweat bee are all to be respected and left alone as their stings can be very painful.

---

[1] Do not use turpentine, rubbing alcohol, or other "smothering" techniques. It can cause the tick to "vomit" which is how pathogens can be transmitted. Also do not use it as a cleanser.

pack rat

Screech Owl

Tortoise

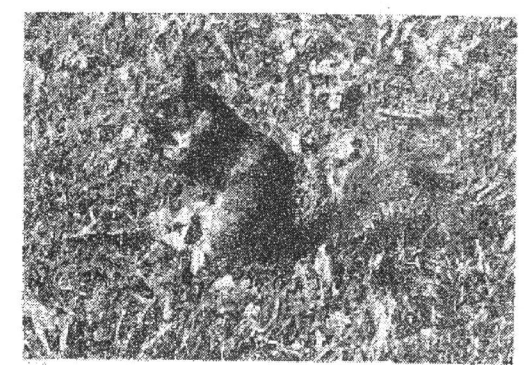
Gray Squirrel

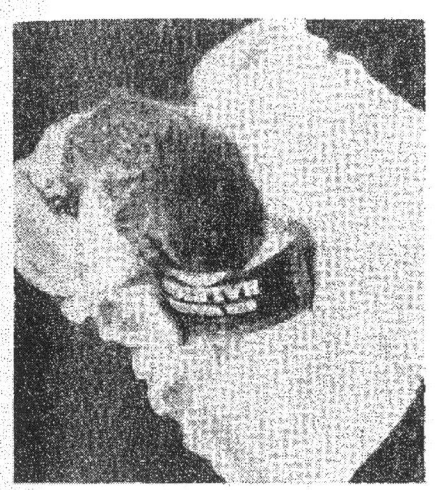
Groundhog(young)

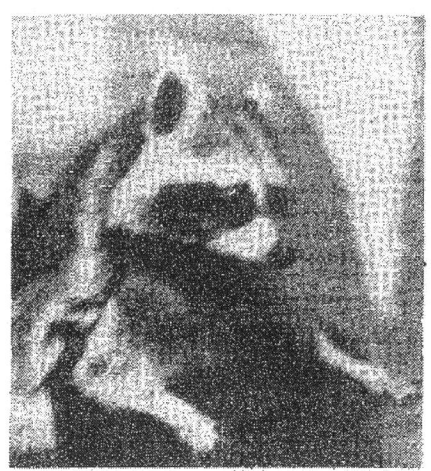
Raccoon

MARINE LIFE:

There are six of More common native Ozark frogs but a half dozen other species may be found in the park. The six best known are: The Bullfrog, Green Frog, Gopher Frog, Wood Frog (tree frog), Leopard Frog and the Pickeral Frog.

The eggs of the frog are deposited in great masses in shallow water. Upon hatch— the babies appear as tadpoles. Many mammals, birds, and fish feed on tadpoles. Frogs produce music or the camper during the evening hours. Frog legs are considered a great treat in the float camp.

Toads are the dry land cousins of the frogs. Several species of the toad appear here. Toads live in gardens and dooryards. Their diet consists of insects.

Hellgrammites make excellent fish bait, especially for taking smallmouth bass. It is believed that these strange little creatures are a specie of sea animal which has survived through eons of time to remain with us. The frightful looking creatures are from two to three inches long with sharp little feelers. They can be found under rocks along the riffles.

Crayfish are the vicious looking animals usually found by turning over rocks near the shore. They have two rough front pincers which they can manipulate quite effectively upon the enemy. Crayfish make good bait.

Minnows are tiny fish that live in schools and appear near the surface and along the shore.

Waterdogs or salamanders are the slick appearing lizard type animals that may be found in marshy spots and along the banks of streams. They are also found in underground caves. There are several species of the salamander with various color combinations.

Turtles live in and near water, feasting on both plants and animals. The tortoise or land turtle dwells on land. Both have shells into which they can quickly withdraw from society. A few of the water turtle species have soft shells. Their meat is often eaten by the natives.

Most visitors are happy to know that fishing is allowed within the park subject to lawful regulations. The Most important fish to be taken from the Ozark Riverways are: Black, White, Yellow, and Rock Bass, Crappie, Pike, Jack Salmon, and various kinds of perch and catfish. Trout fishing can be enjoyed on the Eleven Point and at Montauk State Park.

REPILES:

Many species of snakes live in this area. Only a small number are poisonous.[2] They are the Copperhead, Hill Rattler, Wood Rattler, Pigmy Rattler, and the Cottonmouth. The Copperhead is our Most dangerous snake for it gives no warning before it bites. It selects to live anywhere in the hills, except right in the water. The rattlers all have a warning rattle but do not always rattle before biting. The Cottonmouth lives in and near water. Both the Rattlesnake and Copperhead are slow Moving snakes while the Cottonmouth Moves swiftly, strikes rapidly and is gone almost instantly. The Pigmy and Wood Rattlers make a faint buzzing sound while the Hill Rattler gives plenty of warning in a loud noisy rattle. Wear heavy shoes or boots in the woods and around the camp at night. If bitten, apply an ice pack at once and leave on the wound until a doctor can be reached (see biblio. Page 74).

BIRDS

There are many birds living within the park. Many others stop here on their migration routes during spring and fall.

The Most common birds to be seen along the waterways are the green heron and the kingfisher. In the fields the quail, meadowlark, crow, and blackbird predominate.

The common little songbirds such as the wren, bluebird, cardinal, killdeer, chickadee, robin, goldfinch, and oriole live near the farmsteads for protection.

Camp robbers include the jaybird, sparrow, woodpecker, flicker, and catbird. They spy on you while you're cooking and precede to help themselves once you're a few steps away.

The mourning dove is one of the most graceful and charming birds to be seen in the park. Their Mournful calls is considered the first sign of spring. The pileated woodpecker is a large bird that attracts considerable attention.

---

[2] Snakes are venomous. It is a matter of the delivery system, if it is injected its venom, poison is absorbed or ingested.

The very large birds are the wild turkey, hawks, owls, buzzards, eagles, ducks, and cranes. Wild geese appear at migration seasons, but seldom nest or winter in the park.

The Mockingbird mimics the calls of other birds and other animals adding notes of his own. On Moonlight nights the Mocker pours out his melodies while the rest of the world tries to sleep. The catbird is also a Mocker with a melodious song besides his "catlike" calls.

The eerie little screech owl has frightened man Ozark visitors. The whip-poor-will and its cousin the Dutch whip-poor-will are plentiful in the park and may be heard anytime between sundown and sunup. They may be seen along roadways by night.

Bobcat

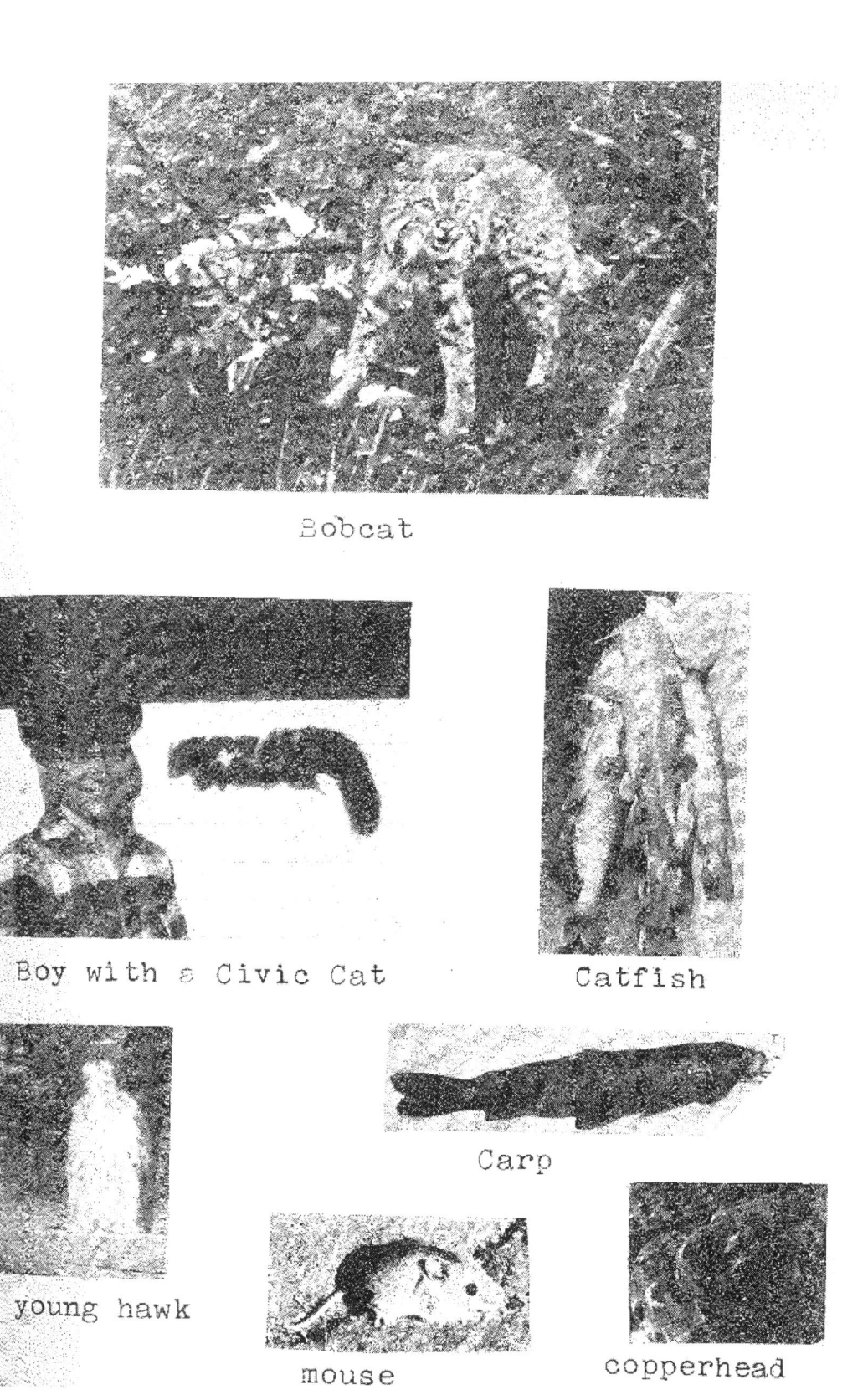

Boy with a Civic Cat

Catfish

Carp

young hawk

mouse

copperhead

History

The "Bluff Dwellers" is the name applied to the folks who are believed to have lived between 8,000 and 10,000 years ago under the bluffs in this area. We do know by the relics found here that some Indians lived under the bluffs, or at least camped there much More recently.

These people were great weavers. They used wild hemp for making blankets, and fish nets. Spear throwers have been found which indicate that these people were here prior to the invention of the bow and arrow.

Bird claws, bear claws, boar tusks, rattlesnake rattles, and oyster pearls were worn as trinkets to prove hunting ability. Giant fishhooks have been found as well as miniature tomahawks. Both are believed to have been good luck charms. Chipped stones in the form of tiny snakes, thunderbirds and chunky stones have been found. These were used in ritual ceremonies. Indian youths made turtle shell rattles by drilling holes round the edges of the shell and attaching hoofs from deer so that they would bump against the hollow shell to create a rumble as the person wearing it walked.

Prior to the white man's appearance here we know that the Ozarks was used as a hunting ground for several tribes including the Osage, Missouris, Shawnees, Delewares, and Choctaws.

From the evidence left by these people and the records left us by the early explorers and hunters, we have placed together a scant history of these people who are without doubt, part of our ancestors. To understand many of our own customs and traditions we must consider those handed down to us from this source.

When we think of the Indians here in our own hills, our first assumption might be that they named many of our rivers and Mountains. However, this is not true. Their place names were soon forgotten or never know to the white man. The white man named Most of the rivers and Mountains. Some were named after Indians, such as Shawnee, Indian, and Deleware creeks. Cardareva Mountain was named for a famous Indian chief of whom the first white settlers heard about. The town of Winona carries the name of a beautiful Indian girl named Winona Norton.

On Cardareva Mountain is the chief's burying ground. He was of the Choctaw tribe, which drifted up into these parts to hunt. Great tribes of the Choctaws inhabited the region around Puxico, MO. This tribe practiced the custom of cleaning the bones of their dead and placing them together with others who had previously died, in earthen caves. The name Choctaw meant to the Indians "separation" for they had separated from the Muskhogean tribe before they migrated north.

The chieftains or leaders of the Choctaws were called Mingoes by their people. It is for this reason that some stories of today relate tales of the Mingo tribe. Actually, the Mingoes were a ruling class of the Choctaw tribe.[3]

Indians made much use of paint. Archeologists believe they made their paint by grinding hematite and mixing it with a liquid which was possibly grease from animal fat. It is believed by the natives here that ingredients for Indian paint was taken from the bluffs in the vicinity of Paint Rock.

FOODS

A mixture of green corn and beans cooked together was called msiquatash by the Indians but now known here as succotash.

The squaws made bread by stirring cornmeal, salt, and boiling water into a mixture which was baked in small cakes on top of flat hot rocks. Sweet cakes were baked in the same way from a mixture of cornmeal mixed with persimmon pulp. Dried persimmon pulp could be kept for weeks.

Making the cornmeal was quite aa chore for the squaws. It was necessary to pound the corn for hours in large rock basins. Hominy, known by the Indians as authuminia was made from corn. Today this simple method is still used to produce one of the fine Ozark food products.

The Indians placed corn grains in boiling lye water. The lye was obtained from wood ashes. The hard outer skin of the corn grain soon became soft. It would begin to break and separate from the inner kernel. The corn was then placed in a basket which was dipped up and down in clear, cold water until the lye and corn skins were removed. The kernels were then boiled until soft enough to eat. Hominy kept well during the winter without canning. For that reason, it proved to be a very important food for the early settlers too.

---

[3] There actually is a Mingo tribe, located in the Ohio Valley. There is historical evidence that Choctaws did refer to the major spiritual and tribal leaders as Mingoes though.

Sagamite was another sweet treat made from corn meal and maple syrup. Traveling Indians, such as warriors, carried only a small sack of parched cornmeal. A variety of concoctions could be made, depending upon the food supplies obtained along the way. If no other food was available, the parched cornmeal was mixed with water and eaten.

Indians often cooked beans and meat together in a pot of boiling water. The Ozark families of today often cook the same food in much the same way. Soup was a favorite dish. It was prepared by tossing all the vegetables, meat, and salt along with corn into a container of boiling water. Each person had his own bowl and spoon for which he was responsible.

Meat, of course, was the Indians main food. It was supplied by the braves. However, the squaws did the skinning and preparation. Almost any kind of wild meat or fowl was devoured. When food supplies were scant the children often caught lizards, grasshoppers, and even fishworms for food. These were eaten raw as soon as they were caught.

The squaws prepared the meat of larger animals by boiling, baking, or roasting. Small pieces or individual servings were often wrapped in green leaves to be baked among the coals by the individual to suit his taste and appetite. Whether he preferred to wrap his meat in oak leaves or in hickory was a matter of opinion.

A huge piece of meat such as a deer quarter, was often suspended by a throng over the fire. It was sometimes tied to a limb or to a pole set up "fishing pole" fashion. The meat was always placed on the side away from the smoke to roast. A piece of wood, resembling a crude triangle, was tied to the throng about midway between the pole and the meat. This wood caused the meat to keep up a continuous turning over the embers. A bowl was set under the meat to catch the drippings. Grease in any form was precious to the squaws.

Besides being used for food, the grease and used to apply on Moccasins, leggings, and jackets to help preserve and waterproof them.

The Indians made use of wild fruits, nuts, and acorns for food. Acorns were looked upon with disdain, so long as other food supplies were plentiful. Mixed with suet the acorns of the white oak species were eaten in autumn. Those of the black oak and red oak were eaten after they had been frozen several times. The freezing killed the bitter taste of the dark acorns.

A wild vegetable resembling the sweet potato and known as pash-e-quah, was often eaten by the Indians. Herbs of various kinds played an important role in the Indian's diet and for medicine.

It was an Indian custom to brew various kinds of teas. An herb remedy was used for almost every ailment. Many of these are still in use today such as, the use of slippery elm slime for drawing infection out of sores that were once known as blood boil. Pokeroot juice was for killing the itch parasite. A salve made from poke root juice, suet, and sulphur proved to be even better as a remedy. Mullen tea was used to sooth the nerves as well as to correct female disorders. Various kinds of leaves were pulverized and smoked in pipes to cure coughs. Sassafras tea was believed to have a thinning effect on the blood. A species of the mint plant called dittany, was used for upset stomach and for diarrhea.

Ointments were made by mixing suet with pine tar and various herb concoctions for use in the treatment of rheumatism, sprains, and insect bites.

Many of the old Indian remedies are not to be scoffed at for older folks now living here are positive that they had cures for simple skin cancer, trachoma, and goiter. Some of the medicine men who knew these remedies kept them secret so many of the old receipts have long been lost.

The medicine men used various kinds of magic along with their pots of tea.

Students of Indian lore now believe that much of the casting away of evil spirits was a type of hypnotism used by the Indian doctors. The Monotony of the dance, the similarity of the cadence in the chant, the pungent odor of herbs, smoke and mystic surroundings all aided in the hypnotic affect.

Being disturbed by the coming of the white man, there was a lot of migration among the Indians. The Ozarks served as a hunting ground for various tribes. It was a place of recluse for wandering tribes and homeless bands. Early French explorers saw some Osage Indians camped at Big Spring, but their homelands were farther north. Other tribes also hunted here but lived elsewhere. The Quapaw Indians inhabited the southern Ozarks until 1824 when they ceded their land to the United States.

The Shawnee and Deleware Indians were brought into Missouri shortly before 1800 by a Spanish governor who established them near St. Genevieve and St. Louis to form a buffer state against the More savage tribes in the west. Many of these Indians drifted into this section of the Ozarks to hunt and fish. Between 1815 and 1832 these people sold their territory to travel on westward.

Some of the Mingoes of southeast Missouri came from their swampland homes to live here. These people Moved west and northward along the Old Indian Trail. This old trail is still visible in places. It is located mainly in Carter County, that is, the part that can still be followed. This trail was once the well-known and traveled pathway that was spoken of as "leading from the waters of Current to the waters of Black River." From a point near Van Buren, it follows the north bank of Current River just below the summit of the ridges. It can be seen near the Mouth of Six Inch Hollow and again where it ascends Granite Quarry Mountain on the north side of Schoolhouse Hollow. It follows the divide between Laddie Valley and Beaver Pond Hollow past the Pennington Pond and across Aldridge Valley. The trail completely avoids the "sky line" but affords a view of the valley below.

Along this same trail came the early pioneers, the traders, the trappers, the outlaws, the soldiers, and the lumbermen. The Indian wars had a great deal of influence on the settlement of this particular part of the Ozarks. For years it was a "no man's land" to the Indian tribes. It was chiefly a hunting ground, but it was also used as a battle ground perchance two of the warring tribes happened to be hunting or by an accident met up in the hills. During the first half of the 19th century, it was a land to be feared. It was a wide expanse of lonely wilderness territory filled with wild animals, snakes, and warlike Indians. Only the bravest of hunters penetrated the area. A few small villages did exist, but it was miles between them.

Chief Cardareva lived after the white men came to America in the time of our exploration in the west. A great Mountain in the Current River Valley bears his name.

For many years, in fact, for over a century the Mountain was considered "haunted" ground where our own people dared to go. Only a few hunters braved the secluded hills to search out the possible treasures buried here. These people of the Choctaw Tribe (see page 40) had a strange way of preparing their dead for burial. The story of the "haunted" Mountain was circulated by our early settlers and the hunters. There were phantom ghosts living on the north side of this great Mountain for at night a great flashing of lights could occasionally be seen there striking out among the peaks. The same phenomena have been known to occur on other nearby Mountains. Scientists have not yet explained why these strange lights appear but there is no basis to connect their appearance with the long dead Indians. The old-timers who did not believe the tales about the "haunted" Mountain claimed they were "mineral lights." The lights are now seldom seen but they are still talked about.

This cluster of Mountains are located between Indian Creek and Chilton's Creek on both sides the Current River. Besides the famed Cardareva Mountain, there are Stegall, Big Thorney, Little Thorney, Round Mountain, and the Brandyweed. Viewed from afar these Mountains usually appear to have a halo of purple haze clothing their uppermost peaks. Stegall was named for a once famous hunter and the Brandyweed takes its name from a nearby stream.

Immediately after the Louisiana Purchase of 1803, a lone, explorer, a close relative of Thomas Jefferson, came into the Ozark region on a mission to mingle with the Indians. The man was Pocahontas Randolph, named after the Indian princess, whom he was also related too. He recorded that he found "an underground river" flowing out beneath a Mountain, near the south bank of Current River. This was, of course, Big Spring.

For three years he sojourned in these hills, living among the Indians. During his exploring he became fascinated by the area that is now the present site of Pocahontas, Arkansas.

Randolph returned to Kentucky to find that his good wife had died during his long absence. His older sons were married. He brought the sons and their wives and his younger children back to the Ozarks. They settled at Pocahontas, Arkansas. Right away More of his relatives and neighbors came. The town and county were both named after "Poka," as his friends called him. Other relatives and friends of Randolph's had settled by this time in what is now Reynolds and Shannon counties. The men were all hunters and made many trips across this section to hunt and visit in the Randolph settlement in the south. Sometimes they went downriver by boat and returned overland to bear hunt.

One of the old trails that they and many other frontiersmen were to follow as about the same as the one later known as the Bellview and Pocahontas Road. It left Pike Creek in a southern direction at Poca Hollow to wind across the southern wilderness of Missouri.

Old Van Buren court house

Gravestone in the woods

ancient tractor

Right: Prairie schooner or covered wagon.

A one-roomed scho[ol]

hand carved articles   Fancy Ozark log cabi[n]

Early day surface mine shaft

Oak log cabin   Cabin made of pine logs

Early day "hack" pulled by two horses

A rustic stone fireplace

Early day whisky distellery. The jar catches the moonshine.

Crude stone chimney shows how this work stood
long years of use plus the wear by the elements

The great Ozark wilderness remained virtually unsettled during the latter part of the 18th century. A few Revolutionary war soldiers braved the wilds to penetrate the forest, but they were seldom joined by others. The wilderness was a no man's land while the Indian wars raged. With the advent of statehood for Missouri a semblance of order began to prevail.

The New Madrid earthquake had driven some settlers north and west into our region. Also a few white hunters had taken Indian women and were settled here by 1820. Early records show that a few people from the east had reached this section by 1810 but very few stayed. Some of the early settlements were Chilton, located on Current River below Van Buren; Good Hope located about one and half miles east of Fremont at the junction of Big Pike Creek and Little Pike Creek and the Irish Wilderness. Dagonia and Barnsville, now Ellington, were among the first settlements in Reynolds County. In Shannon County Eminence and Rat were among the first settlements. Cardareva was originally an Indian community as was Shawnee and Indian Creek.

The thirty years prior to the Civil War brought people into the hills who were seeking a place to farm, as well as a place to hunt. The settlements grew and the trails developed into roads. River traffic became less treacherous and wild animals less dangerous.

Communities grew around the trading post, the water powered mills and at river junctions. Furs, herbs, and wild honey were bartered for salt, lead, and medicine. The blacksmith shop was an important place in any community. Gunsmiths and wheelwrights were looked upon with great esteem.

Tobacco was a luxury for a while and was used as a medium of barter. Snuff was used extensively and appealed especially to the women.

The Civil War caused many people to leave the Ozarks for security in the cities. Except for the few settlements it was again a "no man's land."

A large camp, first occupied by southern soldiers, and later by northern troops was located at Van Buren. The present Forest Service Headquarters now occupies the site of the camp. Their rifle range was near where the Rose Cliff Hotel now stands. From all indications northern troops were sent here to occupy an abandoned camp of the southern soldiers so that this section would be in control of the Union.

A battle was fought in the vicinity of Kegsville, and the home of Mary Ann Snider was used as a temporary hospital. A replica of that cabin and its furnishings is now a museum on the courthouse square in Van Buren. This restoration was accomplished by the Carter County Historical Society during the year of the Carter Count Centennial of 1959.

After the war, the settlers returned, and a long period of agricultural expansion took place. At the turn of the century the big mills Moved in to harvest the native timber. With the Timberworks the railroad came, followed by better roads, the automobile, and mechanized farm machinery.

During the timber boom the largest sawmill in the world at that time was located in the town of Grandin. Other big mills were located at West Eminence, Winona, and Angeline. World War I and II brought More changes. Industry Moved in. Reforestation came about along with wildlife conservation. State parks were established, and tourism appeared.

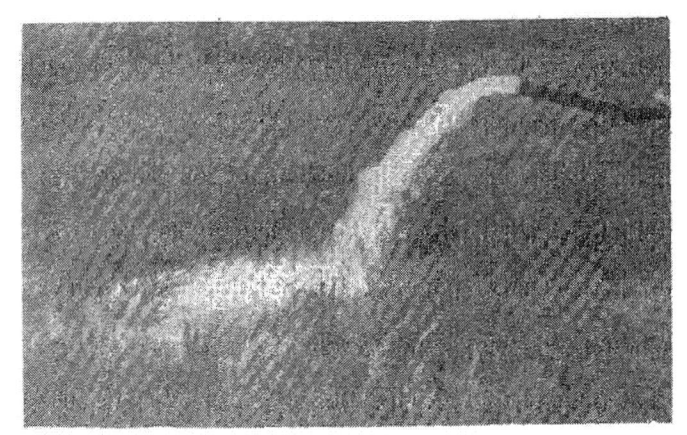

Where Current River begins at Montauk Spring.

Lower level of Rocky Falls

Current River near Booming Shoals

Places in the Park

THE SCENIC RIVERS

Some unusual places, because of their nearness to the river or because of their exceptional scenic value, will be a part of the Ozark National Scenic Riverways. Every mile of the river presents a panoramic view unlike the one before or the one to follow.

Rocky Falls located on lower Rocky Creek.
A creek flowing over a mountain makes a most unusual picture. In rainy season the roar of the falls can be heard for a distance of 6 mi

CAVES

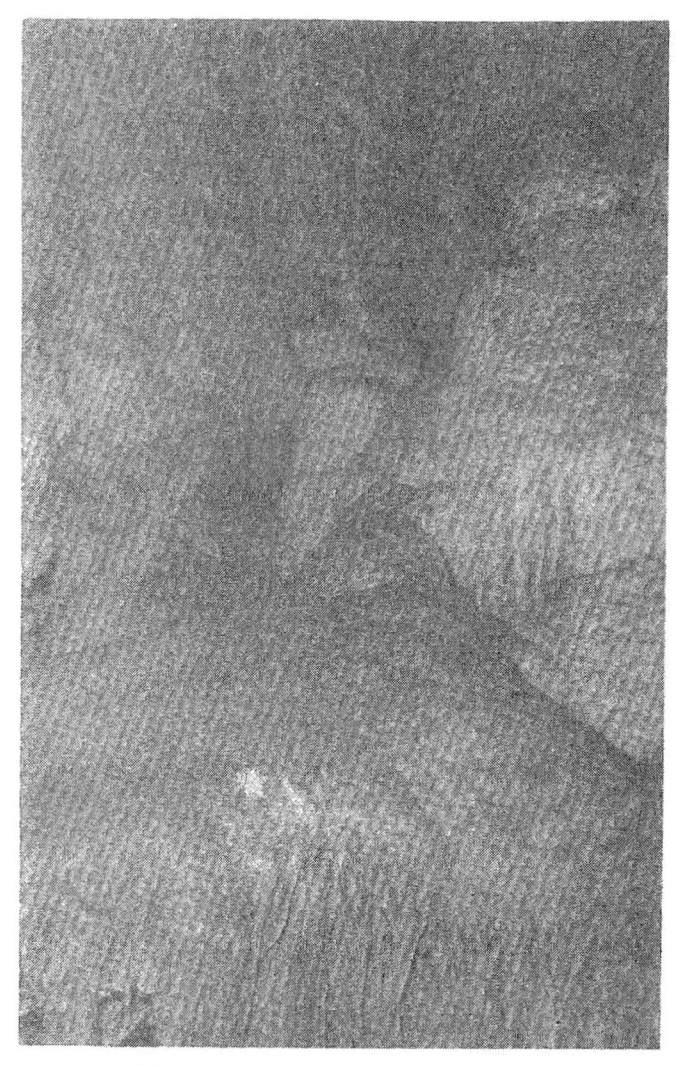

INTERIOR OF AN OZARK CAVE

The caves of the Ozarks provide a place where the visitor can see some of the most unusual works of nature in the world today.

Here in the solitary darkness below the earth's surface are many unbelieveable and fantastic sights.

A fine example of an Ozark Cave maybe seen at Round Springs Cavern just off Highway 19 near Round Spring.

In winter ice sheets sometimes appear in the Ozarks. When this happens the forest and fields resemble a fairyland for a short period of time. An ice sheet is produced by a quick change in temperature that causes the rain to freeze into ice before it drips from the trees. Fog rising near the streams may produce the same effect upon a quick change in temperature.

Recreation

The Ozarks are virtually becoming a playground for the entire Midwest. Just as it once served as at hunting ground for the various Indian tribes it now serves as a hunting place for the surrounding communities. Because of its great forest environment, the low squatty hills, the vast water supplies, and its agreeable climate it is an ideal place to hunt.

Fishing too, is a great sport along the streams. In and around the park are many good places to fish. The area offers many types of fishing—from bank fishing to deep lake fishing. Float fishing on the swift streams is the Most popular.

Float trips are arranged for locally on private rental and guide basis. That is, unless you have your own equipment and act as your own guide.

Nearly all other types of water sports are possible. Canoe trips, as well as the races are very popular. Swimming, water skiing, and floating are all participated in. Folks find joy in shell hunting and the study of the unique marine life. Underwater exploration is going on by deep water divers. This is a relatively untouched area, and the findings of these divers may prove to be of great significance.

Hiking is enjoyed by a great number of people. Many foot trails are to be marked for those seeking this healthful type of recreation. The Ozark region is a good place to hike. The elevations are not extremely high, so that walking is not the difficulty that it is in some Mountain areas.

Good shoes are recommended because of the rough stones to be reckoned with. During the warm seasons poisonous snakes[4] are often seen in the park. Hikers should be careful to stay on or near marked trails as it is not uncommon for strangers to become lost here.

Horseback riding in and near the park may be participated in. Several miles of trails have been planned specially to accommodate this type of recreation. Horseback riding can be enjoyed within the park and also on many other trails in the surrounding area.

---

[4] See note on page 37.

The National Forest Service has provided many facilities for the use of the trail rider. Ask about the Blue Ridge Corral and the Blue Ridge Trail when you are in the Van Buren area, if you have your own horse and equipment.

The National Saddle Trail crosses this area in a south westerly course and is marked for the rider's convenience. Many planned trail rides and horse shows are held here each summer. The Ozarks is the scene each year of the National Trail Ride which consumes an entire week of "living it up in the saddle."

Square dancing is still enjoyed by the hill folks and their visitors. The summertime is a fun filled holiday featuring "homecomings" and country style picnics. You will enjoy the carnival atmosphere of these gatherings.

Hunts mean a great deal to the natives here. The older men and those who like quiet sports enjoy fox hunting. They do not chase after the hounds as is done in the east or in England. They gather around a campfire to listen to the musical notes of the hounds in chase.

The young and vigorous "coon hunt." During the winter, the raccoon may be taken lawfully with dog and gun. During the summer there is a planned hunt nearly every weekend. There are many active clubs that sponsor these trail hunts, water races, and bench shows.

Riding for pleasure

Scene at a national horse show

Current powered ferry-boat on Current River

Floating can be fun and very relaxing

There are many interesting places to see that are not included within the Riverways at this time. The state parks are not yet a part of the National Park. Alley Spring, Big Spring, and Round Spring are all marvels of nature that the visitor will not want to miss seeing.[5] Montauk Sate Park is another beauty spot. The scenery there is nice besides, it is interesting to visit the fish hatchery there. Most of these state parks offer marked nature trails, souvenir stands, camping and picnic areas, beaches, and museums.

---

[5] In 1969 Alley, Big, and Round Springs were donated to the National Park Service to create lynchpins for Ozark National Scenic Riverways.

MARK TWAIN NATIONAL FOREST

The Ozark National Scenic Riverways along the lower Current River in Carter County borders the great Mark Twain National Forest. This section of the giant forest includes about 5000 acres lying in the region of the Ozarks known as the Irish Wilderness. The Current River runs southward across the eastern edge of the wilderness area. The Eleven Point River crosses the southwestern corner. There are many other free flowing streams, lakes, and ponds within the area of the Mark Twain National Forest.

The headquarters of the Mark Twain National Forest is located in the Wilhoit Building in Springfield, MO. There are three ranger districts near the park located at Winona, Doniphan, and Van Buren. The National Forest Service provides various camp sites and picnic areas for visitors. They invite the public to make use of supervised facilities. These facilities are: Watercress Spring, Skyline Drive, and Blue Ridge Horse Trail and Corral; Hawes Memorial Camp Ground; Fremont Tower Roadside Park; Camp Five Pond; Float Camp Recreation Area and Ripley County Lake.

Two other recreational areas that are within easy excess are: Lewis Lake, one and half miles north of Winona on Route 19 and Mill Lake, nine miles northeast of Van Buren just off Highway 21.

A SCENE AT ROCKY SHUTINS

Surroundings

Old Klepzig millhouse on Rocky Creek

Part of the millpond

Below the dam and millpond

Bobcat Cliffs inside Peck Ranch Wildlife Preserve

Granite Quarry on Current River below Van Buren.

Scenic view of Current River looking upstream from the mouth of Jesse James Cave. This cave located across the River from Big Spring, was supposed to have been a hide out for robbers. The cave is rather small but a few men and horses could have been hidden there. A huge rock conceals the doorway but affords the watchman this view of the river.

Round Spring located on Highway 19 north

Blue Spring near Current River below Powder Mil

Alley Spring flows from under a great cliff to form a calm round lake.

The old springhouse has almost disappeared from the Ozark scene. In earlier days the springhouse was an essential part of the farmstead. Now with modern refrigerators and deep freezes both the springhouse and the smokehouse have vanished without hardly a trace fo their earlier existence.

Places of Interest

Big Spring Museum

Boyer's Gift Shop, Highway 21 east

Current River Regional Library- Van Buren (V.B)

Ellington Library

Fremont Lookout Tower and Park

Grandin Community Center

Greer Spring, Highway 19 south

Log Cabin Museum on Van Buren courtyard.

Old Red Mill at Alley Spring State Park

Ozark Country Store, Highway 19 north

Peck Ranch Wildlife Preserve

Phillips Clock Shop near Van Buren

Pink Turquoise Gift Ship, Van Buren

Powder Mill Ferry, Route 106

Riverways Opera, Big Springs

Round Spring Caverns, Highway 19 north

Sassafras City, Highway 60 west of V.B.

Senior Citizen Center, Van Buren

Skyline Drive near Van Buren

Watercress Spring near Van Buren

Park Formation

A great deal of credit is due those who helped make Ozark National Scenic Riverways possible.

In 1964 when final action was taken by Congress to make the Ozark Riverways into a National Park, Lyndon B. Johnson was President of the United States. John M. Dalton was then Governor of Missouri. United States Senators were Stuart Symington and Edward V. Long. Representative in Congress for this area was Richard Ichord.

State Senators were: Earl R. Blackwell and Nelson B. Tennin.
State Representatives were: W.T. Bollinger, Jr., Carter County; V.M. Baltz, Shannon County; Dorman L. Steelman, Dent County; James Cordell Skaggs, Reynolds County; and Earl L. Sponsler, Texas County.

The Ozark National Scenic Riverways first advisory commission were:
Leonard Hall, Caledonia, Mo.
Anthony Buford, Clayton, Mo.
Carlton Bay, Salem, Mo.
Earl Buffington, Summersville, Mo.
Carl Seaman, Eminence, Mo.
Coleman McSpadden, Van Buren, Mo.

The first national park superintendent here was Ed Davenport, followed by Vernon Hennessey who is in charge now. The chief ranger is Richard R. Youse.

BIBLIOGRAPHY

Bretz, Harlem, *Caves of Missouri,* Geological Survey & Water Resources Rolla, Mo.

Centennial Commission, *Civil War in Mo. 1861-1865.* (Pamphlet)

Collins, Earl & Snider, Felix, *Missouri.* Midland State. Webster Pub. Co. 1955, $2.75

Hall, Leonard, *Stars Upstream,* University of Chicago Press. 1958 $2.63.

Keller, W.D., *Common Rocks and Minerals of Mo.* Mo. Handbook No. 1, .35 cents.

Oakley, Eugene, *History of Grandin,* Gene Oakley, Van Buren, Mo. 1963. $1.00

Pennington, Eunice, *History of Carter County,* Penningtons, Fremont, Mo. 1959. $1.00

Pennington, Eunice, *History of the Ozarks,* Penningtons, Fremont, Mo. 1963. $2.00

Rickett, Theresa C., *Wild Flowers of Mo.* University of Missouri. .50 cents.

Steyermark, Julian A., *Spring Flora of Mo.* Botanical Garden, St. Louis & Field Museum of Natural History. Chicago 1940. $3.00.

Swartz, C.W. *Snakes and Facts About Them,* Missouri, Conservation Commission (pamphlet)

"Missouri Conservationists" Mo. Con. Commission, Jefferson City, Mo. Free to Missourians. $1.00 per year outside Mo.

"The Ozark Mountaineer" Branson, Mo. Eleven issues per year $2.00, single copy .25 cents.

Index

acorns 42
agriculture 21
Aldridge Valley 46
Alley Spring 9, 50, 64
anthocyanins 17
asters 17
authuminia 42
badger 24
Barnsville 54
Barren Creek 30
bass 37
bats 33
bear 24, 26, 32
beaver pond 46
bees 34
Bellview 48
berries 21
Big Spring 13, 45, 64
Big Thorney 47
birds 38
blackbird 38
bluebird 38
Blue Ridge Trail 64
Blue Spring 69
Bluff Dwellers 40
bobcats 24, 39, 67
Booming Shoals 56
Boston Range 11
Brandyweed 47
buzzards 38
Camp Five 64
Cardareva 41, 47, 54
cardinals 38
carotenoids 17

carp 39
carrion 26
Carter 9, 46
catbird 38
catfish 37, 39
caves 13, 58
chickadee 38
chiggers 34
Chilton 54
Chilton's Creek 47
chipmunk 29
chlorophyll 17
Choctaws 40, 41, 47
civic cats 24, 39
Civil War 54, 55
Clarksville 15
climate 14
Conservation Comm. 24
copperhead 37, 39
corn flowers 17
cottonmouth 37
coyotes 24
cranes, 38
crappie 37
crayfish 36
crow 38
Current R. 9, 10, 11, 46, 47, 56, 63
Dagonia 54
deer 24, 26
Deleware 40, 41
Dent County 9
Department of Int. 9
dittany 42
dog fennel 21

73

dogwood 17
Doniphan 64
dove 38
ducks 38
eagles 38
Eleven Point 37, 64
Ellington 54
Eminence 2, 54
fawn 25
fish 37
flicker 38
Float Camp 64
flying squirrel 29
foods 42
fox squirrels 31
foxes 24, 32
French 10
Fremont Tower 64
frogs 36
garlic 17, 20
geese 38
Ginseng 16
goldfinch 38
goldenrod 17
Good Hope 54
Granite Quarry Mtn. 46
gray fox 32
gray squirrel 29
groundhog 24, 35
hack 51
Haws Campground 64
hawks 38, 39
hawthorne 17
hellgrammites 36
heron 38

history 40
hogs, wild 27
hominy 42
hornets 34
Huntington 15
Indians 10, 11, 40, 41, 42, 44, 45
Indian Creek 54
Indian Trail 46
Irish Wilderness 54, 64
Ivy, poison 20
jack salmon 37
Jack Fork 9, 10, 11
jaybird 38
Jesse James Cave 68
Johnson, Lyndon B. 9, 73
Kansas City 9
Kegsville 55
killdeer 38
kingfisher 38
Klepzig 66
Laddie Valley, 46
ladyslipper 17
La Honton 11
leach 34
Lewis Lake, 64
linside 15
lizards, 33
Louisiana 48
maple syrup 42
Mark Twain Nat. F. 64
meadowlark 38
Memphis 9
Miller Lake 64
Mingoes 41, 46
mink 24

minnows 36
Missouri 10, 11, 45, 47
Mo. Con. Comm. 7
mockingbird 38
Montauk 9, 37, 56
moonshine 52
mouse 33, 39
mullen 42
mushrooms 20
Muskhogean 41
muskrats 24
National For. Ser. 7, 9, 61
National Horse Show 62
National Park Ser. 7
National Saddle Trail 61
New Madrid Earthquake 54
onions 20
opossum 24
orchid 17
oriole 38
Osage 40
otter 25
Ouachita 11
owl 35, 38
Ozarka 8
Ozark Mountains 9
Ozarks 8, 11, 12, 16, 17, 18, 21, 24 ,25, 29, 36, 40, 43, 45, 54, 55, 59, 61, 64
Ozark National Scenic Riverways 2, 3, 7, 9, 24, 55
Ozark Waterways 37
packrat 33

Paint Rock 41
parched cornmeal 42
pash-e-quan 44
Peck Ranch 19, 67
Pennington Pond 42
Penningtons 78
perch 37
persimmons 42
pigmy rattler 37
pike 37
Pike Creek 48
plum 17
Pocahontas 48
poison ivy 20
poison mushrooms
pokeroot 44
Poplar Bluff 9
Powder Mill 69
prairie schooner 54
president 9
Quapaw Indians 11, 54
rabbits 24
raccoons 24, 27, 35
Randolph 48
rat 33, 54
rattlesnake 37
recreation 60
repestrine 16
reptiles 37
Revolutionary War 9, 54
Reynolds County 48, 54
Rhododendron Roseum 18
Ripley Co. Lake 64
Riverways 9
robin 38

75

Rocky Creek 66
Rocky Falls 56, 57
Rocky Shut-ins 65
Rose Cliff Hotel 55
Round Mountain 47
Round Spring & Cave 58, 64, 69
sagamite 42
salamanders 36
salmon 37
sassafras 16
scientists 13
scorpions 34
screech owl 35
scuba divers 33
Shannon County 48, 54
Shawnees 40, 41, 45, 54
sheep sorrel 20
skunks 24, 28
Skyline Drive 64
Snider, Mary Ann 55
soils 15
sparrows 38
spiders 34
springs 12, 13
squirrels 24, 29
St. Frances 11

Stegall 47
St. Genevieve 45
succotash 42
tarantula 34
tannins 17
Texas County 9
ticks 34
toads 36
tortoise 35
trees 18
trout 37
turkeys 38
turtles 37
United States 9, 4, 5
Van Buren 19, 46, 55, 64
Van Buren Courthouse 49
wasps 34
Watercress Spring 64
waterdogs 36
weasel 24, 33
weavers 40
wild geese 38
wild hogs 27
wild turkey 38
Wilhoit Building 41
woodpecker 38
yellowjacket 34

The Authors

Albert is a recent graduate of the Van Buren High School and will attend the Three Rivers Junior College at Poplar Bluff, Mo. He specializes in the study of wildlife and writes of what he observes. His recent articles have appeared in several magazines including Full Cry, Ozark Mountaineer, and Fur, Fish, and Game. He cowrote this book with his parents Eunice and D.D.

Eunice is the author of several other books (see bibliography page 74). She is a professional librarian and administers the three county Current River Regional Library System.

D.D. a veteran of World War II, is now engaged in farming. Their daughter, Mary, is pictured on page 60-61.

Made in the USA
Monee, IL
17 March 2024